CARMELITE COMPA

Steps of Pain, Steps of Hope

Reflections on the Way of the Cross

by **Matthew Dickens**

Saint Albert's Press
2012

© British Province of Carmelites.

All rights reserved. Except as permitted under current legislation no part of this work may be photocopied or reproduced, stored in a retrieval system, published, performed in public, adapted, broadcast, transmitted, recorded or reproduced in any form or by any means without the prior permission of the copyright owner.

The right of Matthew Dickens to be identified as the author of this work has been asserted in accordance with sections 77 and 78 of the Copyright, Designs and Patents Act 1988.

Artwork by Anne Kelly: www.annekellytextiles.com

Scripture quotations are taken from *The New Jerusalem Bible*, edited by Henry Wansbrough, O.S.B., (London: Darton, Longman & Todd, 1985) © Darton, Longman & Todd Ltd. and Doubleday & Company Ltd.; used with permission.

The British Province of Carmelites does not necessarily endorse the individual views contained in its publications.

First published 2012 by Saint Albert's Press.

Saint Albert's Press
Whitefriars, 35 Tanners Street,
Faversham, Kent, ME13 7JN, United Kingdom
www.carmelite.org
ISBN-10: 0-904849-43-0
ISBN-13: 978-0-904849-43-1

Edited and designed by Johan Bergström-Allen, Carmelite Projects & Publications Office, York.

Typeset by Jakub Kubů, Prague, Czech Republic.
Production coordinated by Karmelitánské nakladatelství s.r.o., Kostelní Vydří 58, 380 01 Dačice, Czech Republic, www.kna.cz.
Printed by ERMAT Praha s.r.o., Czech Republic.

FOREWORD

Many of us were brought up on the *Stations of the Cross* by Saint Alphonsus Liguori. Good as they are, it is also very helpful to read fresh reflections which focus on the mystery of the Passion.

Steps of Pain, Steps of Hope – Reflections on the Way of the Cross by Monsignor Matthew Dickens is a fresh and moving meditation on the Passion of Jesus Christ.

Each station reflects something in our own lives, such as love, uncertainty, compassion, moral weakness, death, Eucharist, prayer.

I warmly welcome these *Stations of the Cross* and hope that they will be read and reflected upon by many Christians.

+ Cormac Card. Murphy-O'Connor
Archbishop Emeritus of Westminster

ACKNOWLEDGMENTS

I would like to thank those friends who have helped me in the preparation of this work: to Monica Hayes for typing the manuscript and to Anne Kelly for her illustrations; and to my mother, Margaret, who nursed me through the period of convalescence when I wrote these meditations.

Matthew Dickens

INTRODUCTION

The Christian journeys through life hoping and yearning for the Kingdom of God, where all pain, suffering and sin will be healed by the reconciling power of God's love.

This journey can never be an easy or straightforward one, since every human being shares in the Fall of Adam and Eve, the rebellion against God that lies so deep in our hearts.

Jesus' journey to the Crucifixion and beyond it into the Resurrection reveals that our Christian hope is not an empty dream. The risen Lord will lead us to his Kingdom, however frail our faith may be and however heavily our sins may weigh us down.

So we make this Way of the Cross with Jesus, now risen and glorified, renewing our faith in his words: "Come to me, all you who labour and are over-burdened, and I will give you rest" (*Matthew* 11:28).

The First Station: Jesus is condemned to death

We adore you, O Christ, and we bless you;
Because by your Holy Cross you have redeemed the world.

> *Pilate asked "But what harm has he done?" But they shouted all the louder, "Let him be crucified!"*
> *(Matthew 27:23)*

As Procurator of Judaea, Pontius Pilate was tasked with the smooth-running of this particularly troublesome corner of the Roman Empire. He needed stability and would have it, whatever the cost. Although in his conscience he knew that Jesus was an innocent man, to avoid civil disturbance he handed him over to the crowd and to certain death.

In the exercise of authority, it is often easier to choose the politically expedient solution rather than to stand up for justice and truth. Our minds can find all sorts of ways to justify the evasion of truth. When we do this, we are no better than Pilate washing his hands. We have failed to take responsibility.

Pause

Lord, forgive the abuse of power in whatever form it takes. Give us courage to stand up and be counted, to defend the innocent and marginalised. You will call us to account for what we say and do: strengthen us, then, to proclaim the truth and justice of your Kingdom.

Our Father ... Hail Mary ... Glory be ...

The Second Station: Jesus takes up his Cross

We adore you, O Christ, and we bless you;
Because by your Holy Cross you have redeemed the world.

> *Carrying his own cross he went out to the Place of the Skull, or, as it is called in Hebrew, Golgotha.*
> *(John* 19:17)

The Roman method of crucifixion was not only physical torture, it was psychological as well. The condemned person was forced to carry the instrument of his own death through the baying, hysterical mob. There was no mercy here, nothing to ease the mind from the physical suffering to come. Jesus was ridiculed, taunted and spat upon: a man deprived of every human dignity as he began his journey to Golgotha.

We recoil at such inhumanity, such grotesque violence. Yet this cruelty exists among us when a child is neglected or abused; or when an elderly person is terrorised and beaten up. These things bring shame on our society.

Pause

Lord, as we see you accept the instrument of your suffering and death, help us to understand how small our sufferings often are in comparison with yours. We cannot make this journey with you except by carrying our share of your cross. Help us to walk with courage, uniting our suffering with yours. Do not let us vanish into the crowd, but strengthen us to stand and protect those who are most vulnerable.

Our Father ... Hail Mary ... Glory be ...

The Third Station: Jesus falls the first time

We adore you, O Christ, and we bless you.
Because by your Holy Cross you have redeemed the world.

He was so inhumanly disfigured that he no longer looked like a man.
(Isaiah 52:14)

It seems that Jesus had not gone very far before falling under the weight of the cross. This is no surprise. He had already been lashed, the flesh of his back opened by the scourger's whip. Blood smeared his face as it ran from the gashes made by the crown of thorns that had been rammed upon his head. No wonder he could not balance the beam's weight on his shoulders, but fell in the dust beneath him. Some onlookers no doubt laughed at this pitiable sight, ruefully recalling that this was the same man who had entered Jerusalem in triumph only a few days before.

Sometimes we feel we have not travelled very far before some persistent sin throws us to the ground again. We leave confession with every good intent, but are quickly depressed by our moral weakness. Jesus' fall reminds us that while his falls were purely physical, he nevertheless knows how hard it can be to lift ourselves out of sins that are deeply ingrained in our lives. We are, then, to find courage and hope in this fall of Jesus, and to know that while we cannot help him stand again, Jesus can help us.

Pause

Lord, help me to raise myself again even if I sin many, many times. Help me to use your sacrament of forgiveness to heal and strengthen me. Let despair not take its hold, but let your humanity encourage me to try again.

Our Father ... Hail Mary ... Glory be ...

The Fourth Station: Jesus meets his Mother

We adore you, O Christ, and we bless you;
Because by your Holy Cross you have redeemed the world.

> *"He has pulled down princes from their thrones and raised high the lowly."*
>
> (*Luke* 1:52)

From the moment of the Incarnation, Mary's life had revolved around her Son. She had borne him, suckled him, nurtured him and comforted him as every loving mother does her child. She had seen him grow into a man and had to watch as his public life led him deeper and deeper into conflict with the religious authorities. Never would she forget the words of Simeon, "a sword shall pierce your own heart too" (*Luke* 2:35). How sharp that sword must have felt now, as she gazed on her suffering son.

We do not know if any words passed between Mary and Jesus in this moment they shared together. Language is often inadequate to express our deepest feelings, and profound love is best shared silently. All Mary's love for her Son was expressed in her eyes as she looked at him, and Jesus knew that his Mother would be with him to the end.

Pause

Lord, I thank you for the people whose love has sustained me, especially in the darkest moments of my life. I entrust them all to your safe-keeping. Help me, and all your Holy Church, to express love with or without words. Bless those whom you call to stand silently beside those who suffer, and let your healing peace flow through them.

Our Father ... Hail Mary ... Glory be ...

The Fifth Station: Simon of Cyrene helps Jesus carry his Cross

We adore you, O Christ, and we bless you;
Because by your Holy Cross you have redeemed the world.

> *They enlisted a passer-by, Simon of Cyrene, father of Alexander and Rufus, who was coming in from the country, to carry his cross.*
>
> (*Mark* 15:21)

Simon of Cyrene was just a bystander who was called out of the crowd to assist Jesus carry his cross. Probably he had little desire to be caught up in this demeaning spectacle and may well have resented being forced to take part in it. Yet Simon's encounter with Jesus so moved him that he became a true disciple and passed his faith to his sons Alexander and Rufus.

We are sometimes called to take responsibilities that we find onerous and daunting, feeling we are not up to the task. We would rather be left alone to carry on as we have always done. Change can disturb our comfort and undermine our sense of security. But we do not know what we are capable of until something we have not chosen to do is demanded of us. Then we can discover that what daunted us is in fact an opportunity to grow in faith. We discover parts of ourselves we never knew existed.

Pause

Lord, when we are confronted with challenges in life that alarm or distress us, help us to see that it is in saying "yes" to life that we discover who we truly are. Help us to shake off our complacency and the fear of change that stunts our growth. May we seize those grace-filled moments that draw us more deeply into your life and that change us for ever.

Our Father ... Hail Mary ... Glory be ...

The Sixth Station:
Veronica wipes the face of Jesus

We adore you, O Christ, and we bless you;
Because by your Holy Cross you have redeemed the world.

> *"Sir", he said, "if you are willing you can cleanse me". Jesus stretched out his hand, and touched him saying "I am willing, be cleansed".*
>
> (*Luke* 5:12)

The name Veronica literally means 'true image'. This refers to the tradition that when Veronica wiped Our Lord's blood-stained face, his image was left on her towel. In another sense, Veronica was *herself* a true image of Jesus because she reached out to him in compassion and love. Her gesture was a brief moment of healing in hours of anguish, and reflected the many times Jesus had reached out to others in their suffering.

Each time we offer a simple gesture of compassion to another person, the image of Christ is truly imprinted in us. This is so even though our lives are distorted by sin. God knows our weakness yet still calls us to bring his love to others through words of encouragement or a gentle touch. In this way we can all be Veronica. Sometimes, too, we need to be humble enough to let others minister to us, to allow them to touch our wounded selves.

Pause

Lord, let all Christian women and men bear the name Veronica. Build up in us a love for others that will show itself in simple acts of healing and compassion, so that we do indeed reflect your face to the world. And give us grace to accept the love that others have for us.

Our Father ... Hail Mary ... Glory be ...

The Seventh Station: Jesus falls a second time

We adore you, O Christ, and we bless you;
Because by your Holy Cross you have redeemed the world.

> *"Behold the Lamb of God who takes away the sins of the world."*
>
> *(John 1:29)*

Even with the help of Simon, Jesus was unable to steady himself enough to avoid falling a second time under the weight of the cross. While Simon could share the physical load of the timber's weight, he could not share with Jesus the burden of humanity's sin. That weight Jesus had to carry by himself, because only he is free from sin. He alone is the Lamb of God who takes away the sins of the world, and only by his death and resurrection could that burden finally be put down.

The spiritual reality of what was happening to Jesus as he staggered to Golgotha is quite beyond our grasp. Our own sins seem bad enough: but the sins of every man and woman from the Fall to the end of time? This is too much for our understanding. It leaves us speechless, but shows us the enormity of the Father's love, that He should give His Son into our hands to suffer and to die for us.

Pause

Lord, the immensity of your love is beyond our comprehension. As I stand in awe at what your Son endured for my salvation, strengthen me and all who profess the Christian faith to live by your commandments. May I love you with all my heart, soul, strength and mind, and my neighbour as myself.

Our Father ... Hail Mary ... Glory be ...

The Eighth Station:
Jesus meets the women of Jerusalem

We adore you, O Christ, and we bless you;
Because by your Holy Cross you have redeemed the world.

"Daughters of Jerusalem, do not weep for me; weep rather for yourselves and for your children."
(*Luke* 23:28)

A group of women gathered at the roadside, weeping at the sight of the disfigured Jesus as he struggled past them. Their sorrow was real, but Jesus told them to weep not for him, but for themselves and for their children. He knew that their grief would be even greater when the persecution of the Roman occupation claimed the lives of their own loved ones.

How many women in human history have had to grieve the violent death of their children! In our own day, terrorism makes no distinction between male and female, military or civilian, adult or child. Even our most sophisticated military technology cannot guarantee safety from the home-made roadside bomb or the suicide bomber. Wherever there is violent conflict, women and men will grieve the loss of loved ones.

Pause

Lord, let your Church speak boldly for reconciliation in our war-torn world. Turn the hearts of men and women of violence to peace, that all people may live without fear of conflict. We are one human family: help us to restore the trust that has been lost.

Our Father ... Hail Mary ... Glory be ...

The Ninth Station: Jesus falls a third time

We adore you, O Christ, and we bless you;
Because by your Holy Cross you have redeemed the world.

> *He had no form or charm to attract us, no beauty to win our hearts; he was despised, the lowest of men, a man of sorrows, familiar with suffering.*
>
> (*Isaiah* 53:2-3)

As Jesus neared the place of execution, he again collapsed under the weight of the Cross. His frame ached with exhaustion but he knew the worst was still to come. It would not be long before the wood that brought him to the ground would hold him in agony above the earth.

We sometimes muse on the manner of our death: will it be a sudden end of which we know little, or a protracted ebbing away of life as disease gradually claims our bodies? Will we suffer pain or slip gently away? Will there be loved ones with us, or will we face the final mystery alone?

Whatever the circumstances of our death, our Christian faith calls us to take each day as an opportunity to grow in love for God. Even the frailest person at the end of life can radiate hope and joy, somehow overcoming the indignity of illness. There is no situation which cannot be used by God to reveal something of himself.

Pause

Lord, when I approach my end, give me courage to place my trust in your mercy and forgiveness. Sustain me by the prayers of your Church, and give me the comfort of the sacraments which will bring the risen Lord to me when my strength has gone. Let me know deep within my heart that you are with me, and that you too have felt your life slip from your grasp.

Our Father ... Hail Mary ... Glory be ...

The Tenth Station:
Jesus is stripped of his garments

We adore you, O Christ, and we bless you;
Because by your Holy Cross you have redeemed the world.

> *Then they crucified him, and shared out his clothing, casting lots to decide what each should get.*
>
> (*Mark* 15:24)

Jesus had now reached the place of his execution and the final acts of degradation were about to take place. The soldiers removed his clothes, stripping him not only of his garments but of the last vestige of his dignity. One is reminded of photographs of the Nazi concentration camps, with prisoners stripped naked and even their hair shaven off. Forced nakedness is a gross violation of the person's right to honour and respect.

The dying hours of the Son of Man were spent in nakedness: naked before God the Father; naked before his mother and the disciple he loved; naked before anyone curious to see the "King of the Jews". We too look on his nakedness, ashamed that human beings can so degrade one of their own kind. If Jesus was forced to show himself to us like this, why do we try to cover up the reality of who we truly are?

Pause

Lord, your nakedness teaches me that I should not try to conceal anything of myself from you. You know who I am already, but so often I am afraid to approach you in my inner nakedness. Give me courage to stand before you as I really am.

Our Father ... Hail Mary ... Glory be ...

The Eleventh Station:
Jesus is nailed to the Cross

We adore you, O Christ, and we bless you;
Because by your Holy Cross you have redeemed the world.

> *When they reached the place called The Skull, there they crucified him and the two criminals, one on his right, the other on his left.*
>
> (*Luke* 23:33)

Jesus had been trained in the carpenter's trade. As a boy he must have often watched Joseph hammering nails into wood, and as he learned his craft he would become familiar with the smell and feel of timber. Now, the materials that had been his livelihood become the instruments of his death. Great iron spikes were driven through his hands and feet, staking him to the wooden beams. Then, pulled up by ropes, he was raised high above the ground.

Torture remains commonplace in parts of the world today, used as a means of punishment or to extract information. Many of those seeking asylum in this country are refugees from state-sponsored torture. They do not always find a welcome here.

Pause

Lord, you suffered one of the vilest forms of punishment ever devised. In this you identify yourself with every man, woman and child who suffers any form of torture. Be with those who dread the opening of their prison-cell door, and strengthen all who campaign against the use of terror and intimidation.

Our Father ... Hail Mary ... Glory be ...

The Twelfth Station: Jesus dies on the Cross

We adore you, O Christ, and we bless you;
Because by your Holy Cross you have redeemed the world.

> *After Jesus had taken the wine he said "It is fulfilled"; and bowing his head he gave up his spirit.*
>
> *(John* 19:30)

On the evening of his arrest, Jesus had celebrated the Passover meal with his disciples. At that Last Supper, he offered them the unleavened bread saying "This is my Body", and the red wine saying "This is my Blood". Under the forms of bread and wine, he gave them the fullness of himself. Deserted now by all except his Mother and Saint John, Jesus truly became the Lamb of Sacrifice, pouring out his life-blood on the altar of the Cross.

Every time we celebrate the Eucharist, we remember and make present the saving death of Jesus. In this sacred act we are caught up in the self-offering of Jesus to the Father, making of ourselves a living sacrifice to the glory of his name. And we are nourished by his body and his blood, the food of eternal life.

Pause

Lord, without your death and resurrection, our dying would be eternal obliteration. With your death and resurrection, our dying becomes the opening to eternal life. At the moment of my death, plunge me in the healing power of your redeeming love that I may journey on to my eternal home.

Our Father ... Hail Mary ... Glory be ...

The Thirteenth Station: Jesus is taken down from the Cross

We adore you, O Christ, and we bless you;
Because by your Holy Cross you have redeemed the world.

> *Neither death nor life, nor angels, nor principalities, nothing already in existence and nothing still to come, nor any power, nor the heights nor the depths, nor any created thing whatever, will be able to come between us and the love of God, known to us in Christ Jesus our Lord.*
>
> (*Romans* 8:38)

The Pietà, the dead body of Jesus held in his Mother's arms, is one of the great images of Christian art. Often Mary is portrayed with great dignity, her depth of faith sustaining her in this moment of profound grief. Yet surely it would be no compromise of faith if, in this most human scene, Mary had felt that surge of pain that shakes our whole body with grief. Her tears and cries came not from any lack of faith, but from the utter love she had for her child.

In the midst of her grief, Mary knew that somehow, somewhere, the death of her son would not be the end of his life. The promise made her by the angel that his reign would last forever could not, she knew, be broken. So she continued to believe, despite the dead-weight of her son upon her lap.

Pause

Lord, in the midst of despair you call your people to believe, to trust, to hope. When the darkness of night tries to overwhelm us, remind us that the light of dawn is not far away. Help us, like Mary, to keep faith until the morning comes.

Our Father ... Hail Mary ... Glory be ...

The Fourteenth Station: Jesus is laid in the tomb

We adore you, O Christ, and we bless you;
Because by your Holy Cross you have redeemed the world.

> *Joseph took the body, wrapped it in a clean shroud and put it in his own tomb which he had hewn out of the rock. He then rolled a large stone across the entrance of the tomb and went away.*
>
> (*Matthew* 27: 59-60)

Joseph of Arimathea was a good man, a member of the Sanhedrin and a secret disciple of Jesus. He requested of Pilate the dead body of Jesus and laid it in his own family tomb. It was an act of noble generosity, to dignify the body of Jesus with Jewish burial ritual and to lay it to rest. Mary of Magdala and other women stayed outside the tomb weeping and praying.

After the Liturgy of Good Friday, a deep silence falls on the Church. It is a time of prayerful waiting, of noiseless anticipation before the Easter Vigil can begin. In those mysterious hours when the corpse of Jesus lay in the tomb, while the women prayed, the seed of new life was germinating, life that would overcome the power of sin and death.

Pause

Lord, your Spirit moves in the depth of our hearts, unseen and unheard. Even death has been transformed by your presence, so there is nothing that you cannot touch and heal. Forgive all that is in me that denies your love, re-form me in the image of your Son.

Our Father ... Hail Mary ... Glory be ...

The Fifteenth Station: the Resurrection

We adore you, O Christ, and we bless you;
Because by your Holy Cross you have redeemed the world.

> *Jesus said, "Mary!", she turned round and then said to him in Hebrew, "Rabbuni" which means Master.*
>
> (*John* 20:16)

In the early hours of the third day, darkness turned to light and death to life. The body of Jesus that had lain in death was suffused again with the power of life; not life that would die again, but a new life that is beyond corruption and death. Still bearing the wounds of the crucifixion, Jesus spoke with Mary of Magdala, who had taken him to be the gardener. Over the next fifty days he would show himself repeatedly to the disciples: talking with them, eating with them, breaking bread with them.

On Easter morning a new, wonderful reality broke upon our world. Sin and death are not triumphant, but have been vanquished by God's love. The Resurrection of Jesus has broken their power, and nothing now can separate us from the love of God. The Church proclaims her greatest joy in the words of the Easter Proclamation: "Be glad, let earth be glad, as glory floods her, ablaze with light from her eternal King. Let all corners of the earth be glad, knowing an end to gloom and darkness."

Pause

Lord, let your Church overflow with Resurrection joy. Let all heaven and earth resound with gladness, for all your promises to mankind have been fulfilled. Break open our hearts that we may be replete with joy, hope and love: a new people who will truly sing your praise.

Our Father ... Hail Mary ... Glory be ...

Conclusion

The first Christians believed that Jesus would return in glory very soon. It was only when this did not happen that the gospels were written down, to record for succeeding generations the memories of Jesus' life, death and resurrection.

We are still living in this "Time of the Church", the time between the Resurrection of Jesus and his second coming. We look forward in hope to the consummation of God's plan of salvation, when all will be made one in Christ. Until then, Christians are to proclaim our Resurrection faith and to build God's Kingdom of peace and justice in this world. We must respond to the needs of our broken world because in baptism our new life in Jesus Christ has already begun. The Kingdom of God is indeed among us.

Making our Way of the Cross unites the suffering of our lives with the suffering of Jesus. He went beyond pain and death into the Resurrection, and if we keep faith we too will be led beyond sin, suffering and death to share His new life. The Resurrection of Jesus will heal us, reconcile us and make us one in Christ. There can be no greater hope, no greater joy.

Prayers for the Holy Father's intentions

Our Father ... Hail Mary ... Glory be ...

The Carmelite Family

The Carmelite Order is one of the ancient religious orders of the Roman Catholic Church. Known officially as the *Brothers of the Blessed Virgin Mary of Mount Carmel*, the Order developed from a group of hermits in thirteenth-century Israel-Palestine; priests and lay people living a contemplative life modelled on the prophet Elijah and the Virgin Mary. By the year 1214 the Carmelites had received a *Way of Life* from Saint Albert, the Latin Patriarch of Jerusalem.

Carmelites first came to Britain in 1242. The hermits became an order of mendicant friars following a General Chapter held in Aylesford, Kent, in 1247. Nuns, and lay men and women have always played a major part in the life of the Order, and have had formal participation since 1452. Over centuries of development and reform, the Carmelites have continued their distinctive mission of living 'in allegiance to Jesus Christ', by forming praying communities at the service of all God's people. The heart of the Carmelite vocation is contemplation, that is, openness to and friendship with God, pondering God's will in our lives.

Like the spirituality of all the major religious orders (Benedictines, Franciscans, Jesuits, etc.), Carmelite spirituality is a distinct preaching of the one Christian message. Carmelites blend a life of deep prayer with active service of those around them, and this apostolate takes many different forms depending on the time and the place Carmelites find themselves in.

Over the centuries 'Carmel' has produced some of the greatest Christian thinkers, mystics, and philosophers, such as Teresa of Jesus (of Avila), John of the Cross, and Thérèse of Lisieux (three Carmelite 'Doctors of the Church'). In the twentieth century, the Carmelite Family bore witness to the Gospel in the martyrdoms of Titus Brandsma, Edith Stein, and Isidore Bakanja.

England boasted the largest Carmelite Province in the Order until its suppression at the Reformation. The British Province was re-established under the patronage of Our Lady of the Assumption in the twentieth century. There are communities of friars, sisters and lay Carmelites across England, Scotland, and Wales. Similar communities exist in Ireland, and throughout the world. The international Order of Discalced (Teresian) Carmelite friars, nuns, and laity is also present in Britain and Ireland. Members of the Carmelite and Discalced Carmelite Orders work, live, and pray together to make up the wider 'Carmelite Family', which seeks the face of the Living God in parishes, retreat centres, prisons, university and hospital chaplaincies, workplaces, schools, publishing, research, justice and peace work, counselling, and through many other forms of ministry and presence.

Further sources of information on Carmelite spirituality include:

John Welch, O.Carm.
The Carmelite Way: An Ancient Path for Today's Pilgrim
(Leominster: Gracewing, 1996).

Wilfrid McGreal, O.Carm.
At the Fountain of Elijah: The Carmelite Tradition
(London: Darton, Longman and Todd, 1999).

Johan Bergström-Allen, T.O.C.
Climbing the Mountain: The Carmelite Journey
(Faversham & Rome: Saint Albert's Press & Edizioni Carmelitane, 2010).

Website of the British Province of Carmelites
www.carmelite.org

Some other titles available from Saint Albert's Press…

Carmelite Bible Meditations Series

John FitzGerald, O.Carm.
Backwards into the Future: Meditations on the Letter to the Hebrews

Joseph Chalmers, O.Carm.
The Sound of Silence: Listening to the Word of God with Elijah the Prophet

Johan Bergström-Allen, T.O.C. & Wilfrid McGreal, O.Carm. (eds.)
The Gospel Sustains Me: The Word of God in the life and love of Saint Thérèse of Lisieux

These and other titles on Carmelite spirituality and history can be ordered from:

The Friars Bookshop	Saint Albert's Press	Edizioni Carmelitane
The Friars	Book Distribution	Via Sforza Pallavicini, 10
Aylesford	Carmelite Friars	00193 Roma
Kent	P.O. Box 140	Italy
ME20 7BX	ME20 7SJ	
United Kingdom	United Kingdom	

☎ + 44 (0)1622 715770   ☎ + 44 (0)1795 537038

E-mail:
bookshop@thefriars.org.uk

E-mail:
saintalbertspress@carmelites.org.uk

E-mail:
edizioni@ocarm.org

Saint Albert's Press
www.carmelite.org/sap

Edizioni Carmelitane
www.carmelites.info/edizioni

LAUS DEO SEMPER ET MARIAE